The Seacunny

GERARD WOODWARD was born in London
in 1961. He has published several prize-winning
collections of poetry as well as four novels, including
I'll Go to Bed at Noon, which was shortlisted for the
2004 Man Booker Prize. His last collection of poetry,
We Were Pedestrians, was shortlisted for the 2005
T. S. Eliot Prize. He is a Professor of Creative Writing
at Bath Spa University.

Gerard Woodward

The Seacunny

PICADOR

First published 2012 by Picador
an imprint of Pan Macmillan, a division of Macmillan Publishers Limited
Pan Macmillan, 20 New Wharf Road, London N1 9RR
Basingstoke and Oxford
Associated companies throughout the world
www.panmacmillan.com

ISBN 978-1-4472-1742-8

9 8 7 6 5 4 3 2 1

A CIP catalogue record for this book is available from
the British Library.

Printed and bound by CPI Group (UK) Ltd, Croydon CR0 4YY

for Suzanne, Corin and Phoebe

'The profits are enormous. There is no business like it in the world, and the whole secret is, it costs nothing to feed the cattle. They grow without eating your money. They literally raise themselves.'

– Judge Sherwood

Contents

The Seacunny

Cow Tipping

At certain times and in certain states
A cow will sleep standing up,

Its knees locked like a deck chair,
The heavy head balanced weightless on a neck

Rigged with frozen muscle.
You can see them (or their white halves,

At least) out there, long
After midnight, standing as still as sheds,

And all facing the same way
As though stalled in the middle

Of a pilgrimage. If you are quiet,
You can walk among them

And feel what it might be like
To live a thousand times faster

Than your neighbours
(If you don't already know).

And you could believe it quite possible
That something as square and as anchored

Could be tipped by the touch
Of a single finger, that they might tip

Each other, like dominoes,
And the whole blue field collapse

Into nothing but shadows
On the grass. Do you think you could do it

After a few drinks, say, could be
Quiet and odourless enough,

Could be as milk-heavy and as lost?
Forget it. And none of this is true anyway.

Flatland

Divorced but with nowhere else
To go, we live our own lives
In the one house – you upstairs
In the triangular bedroom,
With its grace-and-favour wallpaper,
Me in the downstairs granny flat
Our grannies always hated.

We could survive like this
For years, characters in a romance
Of many dimensions
(Fie, fie how frantically I square my talk)
With just a few points at which the planes
Of our lives converge – the whirligig
Washing line which orders our clothes

In dripping concentricity,
The wheelie bin in which our waste
Is sealed in alternating layers,
And the corporation composter
That fills and fills and fills but is never full.
And what is it filled with? The wrung bags
Of our different teas and all the vegetables

We failed to eat, salads as bright
As Italian flags, the peels, plumed carrot tops,
Tonsured poppy heads, cached in secret
And deposited after dark, as if we were ashamed,
Or had a daughter who would berate us
For the wasted energy of being apart.
In daylight once I lifted the lid

To find worms plaited in its rim,
And other microscopia working
With the frenzy of lawyers
At a sickbed. If only we had some
Patch of earth that could use the sweet, black
Product, and not the concrete we'd always
Vowed to lift one day, as if it would

Ever get any lighter.
The ceilings are where the pain gathers
Most. A spider's woven zero catches
Only your footfalls. When you take a shower
I hear rain in another dimension,
And all that wasted water
Falling through the walls.

Allegra

She gave herself away, leaving
Footprints in my snow, like arrows

On the floor of the bargain basement.
She'd played with the skulls

I'd found on hillsides, taking the lower
Mandible of some historic ewe,

Bleating through it – the cheek!
I couldn't prove anything. The snow

Had melted before I could take photos,
Didn't have the shoe to compare,

And by then, other people were involved.
She'd stolen a Vespa, and tore round

The streets on freezing afternoons. At least
I could tell, by her rasp, where she was,

Would sometimes see her flash past
Unhelmeted but with a black velvet scarf

Covering everything but her eyes
Which made her seem (what's the word?) *chaste*.

She went through a fence almost leaving,
Cartoon-like, a self-shaped hole,

Knocked a toddler off his swing
Which brought the rage of every Mum

In the district down upon her.
I still wonder if she felt anything.

Perhaps, like me, she was numb.

The Seacunny

Somewhere in The Levels
A bird table was moved by degrees
Further away from a house.

Inch by inch with the season
It receded, its seeds uneaten,
Even when thirty feet from the back door,

Thirty-two, thirty-three, they were that shy.
What could bring the birds joyously
To this little chalet on a pole

But distance, the would-be feeders
Of birds thought, seeing the promise
Of its golden age recede with it,

Of anti-lions and Snow White-style,
Chore-performing wildlife (titmice
Carrying different corners of a pillow case,

Crossbills hacking down cobwebs
With feather dusters). But further,
Forty feet, fifty feet, a hundred.

Not until it was out past the pot-
Bellied firs and then through the arbour
And beyond the sundial (in fir-shade) down

To the water's edge did something visit.
He saw it through binoculars and called out
"The Seacunny! The Seacunny!"

Dressed in a smock of glue and feathers, with a plastic
Cup dabbed yellow for a beak,
It steered its punt right up

To the jetty. "It's taking the seed!
The Seacunny, the Seacunny,
It's taking our seed!"

Both Ends of the Island

The lighthouse, sitting in a bowl of blue weather,
Is home to Joyce, a single mother of twin girls.

She was the wife of the lighthousekeeper
Until he threw in his lot with the dandyish skipper

Of a whelking vessel that twice a day tacks
Round the point and steers through a gap

In the sea wall to land its muddy cargo of dredged
Molluscs on the quay, then to be simmered

For three hours at a time in kettles the size
Of rain barrels. The girls are of an age now,

And Joyce takes them up the winding stairs to the lamp
Before twilight to watch the whelkers coming in

From their sorry little voyages, and points out for them
The craft that is festooned with flags as if for a regatta,

And from which there is even the sound, some evenings,
Of a merry tune played on a squeezebox.

And what should their answer be? To try and scuzz up
His shortwave and leave him without an eye for the weather?

Or wait for the short days and long nights when he'll need
      their beam
To thread his way between the rocky walls

And then, at the crucial moment, to extinguish the light
And let him wash up against the stone in solid darkness?

Or should they just bear in mind that everything he does
He does in their light, that he will live in it forever

That it will follow him everywhere like the train of a silver dress,
That even if he doesn't know it, he will love them?

The Lady of Epping

Having left her life
Through a daring marriage to live
In a Western city,
Having travelled economy class
Through seven layers of heaven
To land in a mown and gated suburb,
She consoles herself with secret visits
To forests, takes the Central Line
Until she falls off the end
And becomes lost amongst the trees
That are almost good enough.
She has got to know them well,
The timid little forests of London,
With their squirrels and drunks.
Her husband despairs
Though he can usually find her
Sitting on the succulent stump
Of a beech, in her duffel coat
And her Alpine hat,
Sucking the ants
From her fingertips.
They need to talk about it.
They really need to talk about it.
But she always says the same thing.

Prezzo

We are the only table in the restaurant.
The décor is stark, glaring, Kubrickesque.
A meal here could stretch itself into eternity.
We are too many, and closer than we need to be.

Every year a new generation is brought to the table.
Three babies lift cutlery with arms that don't bend,
Take a shocking spoonful of their own reflections,
Then drop them on the floor.

They are as far removed from me
As I am from the great-great-grandfather
I never met, who jumped ship rather
Than strip for the deck bath.

Someone plays a counting game with a little girl
Going hand in hand around the table,
Touching each guest in turn and enumerating them
Out loud, first in English, then French, Dutch, German, Italian . . .

Every year since its invention (Ts'ai Lun, AD 105)
The quantity of paper in the world has increased,
Until now, my cousin-in-law (is there such a thing?) says.
The paperless office has arrived.

Opposite, Woolworths is in its final hours.
Through a glaze of lukewarm food I watch the shelves empty.
Now they are selling the shelves. Now they are selling
The signs that say 'Closing Down Sale'.

The sulphur of a tiramisu does its slow, tipsy work.
There was a cathedral city beyond the coat stand when we arrived.
Everything is both unbearably close and yearningly distant.
And I am as hungry as a bank.

Several Uses for a Trampoline

For the Mitchell family

1

Have you ever seen a man
On a trampoline? Really using it?

He falls like a diver into a pool,
To have his fall broken by his own self

Rising to meet him, passing through him,
Back to the stillness between rising and falling.

But it is effortful falling, you can tell
By his gasps and groans, the way his falling

Self somehow wrestles with his rising self,
As though he is continually

Yanking himself out of a swamp,
Then stands for a moment like Raphael's

Assumption of Christ, no visible means
Of support, casually triumphant over death,

But only for a moment, before he must
Go down to meet himself again.

2

Apples falling in the orchard
Give a similar noise, especially when they fall

Onto the trampoline that someone
Has left under the trees, and which

All the neighbourhood's children
Have licence to use. Sometimes

I find them, mine included,
Sitting as one, as though for

A family portrait, the younger ones
Seated in the olders' laps,

And bouncing together rather
Solemnly, seriously, without any

Apparent effort, rising just a foot
Or so; the tense rebounding of the tarp,

The pulling inward of springs that snap
Shut again with a faint piano twang,

Rising and falling, the rising selves passing through
The falling selves, unlike the apples

Who miss the trampoline and thud into
The grass in such a way they do not

Rise again, at least, not for many years.

3

Where did they come from, the trampolines?
Bed sheets stretched between siblings

To give one of them a birthday to remember?
Are they really the invention of one Du Trampolin

Who crystalized the pratfalls and tumbles of clowns
Into something of elegance and grace?

A device on which to learn anti-gravity?
Here is an astronaut on a trampoline,

Looking down on the small
World of the sprung canvas,

Wondering what it would take
To achieve escape velocity

From an average trampoline.
A comet arriving in our world

Stripped of its fire
Is rudimentary. A chunk of iron.

Falling red hot in the village
Of Fairylawn, Idaho, used

As an anvil at the local forge
For forty years, it was *that*

Square, *that* smooth.

4

The thing is to fail to fall.
Listen to the sound of a real

Trampolinist, twelve stone
Of blood and bone gymnast

And he can't even break
The surface tension of this

Little pond, but finds instead
His whole self crushed

To the point of nothing
Before it is released into

The carnival of anti-gravity.
In the curved space of rubber sheet geometry

He creates a point of density
So great nothing can escape.

5

At first my son was afraid
To go on the trampolines

When we found some on a beach
In Dorset (big sign in red – NO

SUMMERSAULTS). They were
Arranged like a ward

Of hospital beds, unsettlingly so,
But a hospital of the perpetually

Reborn, of children with scissor
Legs, starfish-limbed. Now we

See them everywhere – in back gardens from the train,
Some within protective cages

To cope with the catapult effect.
Someone, somewhere, will one day

Invent the trampoline suit
As the only way to travel,

Others see a wizard's mantle
In an unhooked canvas,

And indeed it is, in effect,
(The trampoline) a bottomless well.

The trampolinist, in an average session,
Will plummet two thousand feet.

6

Barani, Rudi, Randi, Adolf,
The summersaults with twists and half twists

That the children are daring to do
On the trampoline in the orchard,

Picking apples at the same time
(Apple harvest on a trampoline)

So their arms fill as they rise and fall,
Rise and fall, and summersault so apples

Spill, and spin, and radiate
Like catherine wheel sparks.

This is the use of trampolines
I will remember, the broken sunlight

Coming through the trees in a strange
Land, and lighting up my rising

And falling children, and their friends,
And the apples falling,

The new trees rising.

γ2 Delphini-c – The Cuboid Planet

Good to imagine an impossible thing,
This planet, for instance, orbiting

A double star in the dainty constellation
Of Delphinus, a world similar

In size and composition to our own
Yet square, like a die, or cube

Of sugar, a structure gravity could never
Allow to happen nor maintain – would mean

A world of six continents each
At right angles to its neighbours,

Peopled by races of equally
Right-angled opinions.

An ocean with a corner in it,
Triple-headed statues of the Corner Gods

Where three sides meet
And, at points were the edge is most sharp

A vantage upon two lands
Alternating in verticality.

You would fall into one
Only for your fall to modulate

Into a gentle stroll, just as the waterfalls
Quickly give up their fury

And become pools of calm.
You imagine some point in history

When the different sides, so unused
To each other's strange angles and slants,

Put an end to those terrible wars
When cavalry went over the top

In an endless flow of fiery mules,
And all the young men

Were thrown over a cliff, (they are still
Walking today, so the legend goes),

And a geniculated political calm descended
Based solely on the geography of squares.

Now the geese in their Ls and Fs
Cross an elbow of sky

As the suns fandango and light up
Three sides and darken three others.

Think about it hard enough and long,
You'll start getting letters in the mail

Stamped with a binary star postmark
"I have so many questions to ask you.

I cannot believe you inhabit a planet
Shaped like a ball. Gravity couldn't

Allow such a thing to happen.
How could you tell one side

Of your world from another,
How can you live a life

With no edges? How do you
Manage to hang on . . . ?"

In the Electricity Gallery

It makes you think.
How an entire room can pour
From a single light bulb.
You can imagine the lamp hours
Paid for by this early example
Of a pre-payment meter,
A little brute of cast iron
And dials that must have lived
In a real house once. A beastly presence
In an Edwardian cubby hole,
Giving the light that several families
Raised their children by.
Their mean, calibrated, origin of epiphanies.

Recent history, yet I feel as though
I'm walking in a hall of mummies,
Trying to imagine the sort of people
Who lived with these things,
In the brief glare of being alive.

Here is the laughable apparatus
Of an early toaster, the little anvil
That was the first electric smoothing iron.
Round pin plugs. Twisted flex.
A television like a small walnut wardrobe.
Fuses like the switching gear
On the Underground. It's all
So wonderfully dead.

Like the trinkets found in the grave
Of some ancient patriarch;
The currency of the life to come
For him, a comb and a ring to us.
Did they ever even think of this little
Thing under the stairs, vending light
As it fed on their dirty pennies,
That all the time they were there
It was doing the sums of their lives;
Counting, that it never stopped counting?

The Lights

I have never been in charge of so much light,
But in this house there are as many varieties
Of light bulb as there are flowers in the garden;
Thin-stemmed and thick-stemmed
Candle bulbs, screw-in spotlights
(Three different sizes) with their misted
Corneas, pearl bulbs with bayonet fittings,
Two roseate forty-watters that do their thing
Beneath the faux logs of the electric fire . . .
The fixtures themselves are as varied;
Flush recesses for spotlights that pinch
Your fingers when you tamper with them,
Who release their bulbs with a slow,
Grinding rotation that any minute
Might freeze, infuriatingly. Gold-veneered
Swivelling spotlights in the kitchen
That cast our breakfasts so starkly
They seem to stare back at us, blinking.
An octopus of brass in the living room,
A creature of fuss and frippery – with all that
Wiring, all those shades and tat
Still a dim and disappointing radiance.
Unlike our two little refractive chandeliers
That hang in a room that can't live up
To their grandeur, with a ceiling so low
The faceted prisms stroke my scalp
And hold me, for minutes sometimes,

In their motionless downpour.
And we can laugh at the vainglorious
Tastes we have to live with,
The all-conquering ambition of the décor
In a house so old it must, for most
Of its life, have been furnished with shadows.
But in the shops I sometimes fill a bag
With light bulbs like a kid
In the pick 'n' mix, carrying them home
As though they were heavy,
Wondering why it matters, feeling slightly guilty
About having so much in our house
To see with, and always a cupboard
Stocked with rations of their unbearable glass,
Like a hoard that will see us
Through a long time of darkness.

Vice

His weight is a kind of weapon,
Like the tyrant king
You couldn't slay for fear

He would fall on you.
He is the bicep of an iron man
Whose other parts we've lost.

Why did I take him in
That Sunday morning,
Slinking off to the DIY shed

As if to a strip joint,
Collar turned up, embarrassed to find
A young girl on the till,

Trying to conceal him even as
I paid my money, then using two bags
For the walk back, him pulling

The handles to breaking point.
There must have been something
I had to do that only he could help me with.

Did I really plan to make furniture?
Or wooden toys for the kids
Who would have outgrown them

In the time it would have taken me
To plane their splinters off?
Was it to bind books?

It doesn't matter. He's staying put.
I've come to like his sullen, unshiftable
Presence. He could come in useful.

Astronomy

One day we'll remember the telescope
And save it from whatever hell it's in,
Snap the cobwebs off its tarnished hull
And raise it on its own three legs again.

Martin

I had that dream again, the one
In which you were fishing in the drain
That ran round the back of your store,
And kept the Medway fed with tyres and grease,

And I saw the glee with which
You reeled in the things you'd hooked;
This time a robot's drowned anatomy;
An arm slightly rusted with a dark

Bling of snails, its hand, three fingers intact,
Giving, by chance, the diving signal
For OK. Then a foot, an electronic ear
And finally a rigid smile of aluminium and wires

That, blushing, you stashed for ever in a keep net.
You were in your working clothes – shirt
And tie, no jacket, with your name badge pinned
Just above your nipple, or through it

(There was blood). Polished shoes
Defiantly bright and clean in all that mud.
I woke with a start at the thought
Of your cleanliness, Martin, how you were always

The cleanest of our three.
Apart from that one time, the morning after
The Christmas party at the shop
When I discovered you foundering in the frozen aisle.

You were wearing a ballerina's costume then
But were in deathly gravitational throes
Like a bird that's been dipped in an oil spill
And can't, for the life of it, take flight.

Your mascara was running
As I lifted you out of that place,
(Your tutu like whiskers against my cheek).
But not from tears, Martin, not from tears.

Rooftop

He's on the roof again.
Exactly where he shouldn't be.
Who does he think he is?

Perhaps he's just watching the stars.
It's a clear night, and Saturn's in Gemini,
Shining like the bulb someone
Forgot to turn off in the repossessed flat.
Or he could see the Marquis's
Knuckleduster hills from there
And hear his sea lions barking.
He could be doing anything.
Thinking anything, he could
Paint a statement in whitewash
For the world to see, tell us
That the council are Nazis,
That his bank is run
By the descendants of lizards.
He could throw things at us.
A single slate could cleave a skull
Clean in two thrown from up there.
That's what worries me.

An Arrow Shower

They are gathered on the ninety metre lawn,
Their backs to the sun and their shadows unrolled
Like strips of black carpet before them.

Turning side on, they view their future
With an askance, almost over-the-shoulder
Squint, drawing back the finger-cutting string

To an anchor point in the face somewhere
Between the cheek bone and the hinge
Of the jaw. One arm heroically forward,

The other hindwards and up to ear level, the recurve
Limbs of their bows bend back as though a bull
Is lassoed by its horns, and by so doing,

They build muscle into the arrow's skinny shaft
So that, with a little click, it vanishes
In a second. The moment of release passes

As a nervous twitch through the whole body,
An electrical jolt, a moment of imbalance; they could fall
At a feather's touch, before they are earthed again.

They move to the telescopes
Easeled beside them, view other worlds,
Then walk to them across a cosmos of grass.

Why are they such mild men, the paunchy, bearded
Redskin-hearted forty- and fifty-year-olds?
In the clubhouse they sit in silence drinking

Stewed tea from plastic cups, eating stale
Custard creams, making sure everyone puts
Their 10p in the pot. Were the men of Crecy this silent

After battle, in their tents, sipping steak
And counting the hearts and eyes they'd pierced?
A portrait in oils of the founder, a chart of handicaps,

Score sheets, cuttings from the local
Press about the boy wonder who scored more golds
Than any other teen. '*I have no friends at school,*

All my friends are here . . .' The future runs
In one direction only. The arrows are always
Sent from the far end

Where the sun goes down in the afternoon.
In nearly a hundred years
They have killed no one.

Stealing Lead from the Temple

I'll tell you about the night we stole lead from the temple,
No gates, no guards; it was really quite simple.

We borrowed my brother-in-law's flat bed truck
And backed it, no lights, half a mile up the track

To where the temple stood on a spur by the lake.
Killed the engine and put on the brake.

The moon in the water, (or was it a swan)?
We put up a ladder. There was work to be done.

The sheets were held to the joists by hooks
And came out as softly as the pages of books.

As I filled the cup of my bricklayer's hod,
I saw in a niche a little Greek God,

Naked yet chaste, some dryad or other,
Or a Venus or Io, Jupiter's lover.

We got on with our work, folding the metal
So heavy and tough but soft as a petal.

It was strange, in the dark, a little perverse
To be acting like builders, except in reverse.

The truck nearly broke for the weight of our booty
And I felt rather sad for that little Greek cutie.

My partner told me those gods were long dead
And the only God now was the value of lead;

It was a temple of love we'd stripped of its clothes –
Well, just its roof, and they could get a new one of those.

Gomez

1

Gomez writing letters to himself
In stolen urine, from a carafe he keeps,
(Slightly chilled), at his frayed elbow.
As he is writing, a tooth falls
From his mouth like a solitary
Hailstone. "O bleak emissary
Of winter," he writes, "that should go
Rat-a-tat on the hood of my old Chevrolet,
Here you bounce just once on my page".
A little blood follows. Not much.

2

Gomez has been kicked in the face
Which has produced the surprising injury
Of a perfectly square wound in the forehead,
A half a centimetre wide and knocked half in,
Like a little door that has been tentatively opened.
A few strands of his glossy black hair are caught
In it, like strip curtains snagged on a latch.

3

Gomez celebrating his birthday with a cake
Formed by his English mother into the shape
Of the lunar module, very badly, everyone agrees.
It is the heyday of Gomez and of the human race.
We have never climbed higher than this,
The moon has never been so close.
Freeze the moment, Gomez cries,
But too late, the cake is cut.

4

Gomez learning the trombone
For purely anti-social reasons.
On the bus he finds the wielding of the instrument
In its black case the ideal way of swiping,
As though innocently, random members of the public.
He is thrown off a bus only once
By a conductor – not for the swiping, but
For his foul-mouthed behaviour just after.

5

Gomez in long trousers, (well, long for him),
Wranglers, with the W sewn into the back pockets,
Flared like bluebells, and a green t-shirt
Proclaiming allegiance to a University
He has never attended (the Sorbonne).
He tries for a degree in Business Studies
At a polytechnic in the North East
Deciding he has just the right brain
(The door is still there, the little
Square scar), but fails his second year
After a first spent in hopeless pursuit
Of a psychology student called Hazel.

6

Gomez is drunk. Look at him!
He was funny at first, but not now.
He has orange ejecta down his front,
A pee-stain in his groin. He has
Lost a shoe and is clutching, for no
Good reason, a naked Action Man.

7

Gomez on drugs, a syringe in his thigh
As he slumps in the cubicle
Of the betting shop toilet.
Not long to go now, though he is taken
In hand by a black woman,
Teller of the shop, whose church
Forbids her to not help
When confronted with such a sight as this.

8

Gomez in recovery, born again
Into an austere form of Christianity,
Married with five children
And living in Mexico City
In a good job in IT with great prospects.
One day he will jack this all in
And devote himself wholly
To the service of Christ's message,
Take himself and his children
And his beautiful wife
Into the desert and build a church there.

Priddy

'As sure as our Lord walked in Priddy'

If Jesus was a trader in tin,
He may well have come here,
His ingots, sleepy as puppies,
Slung on his damp shoulder.

On the green, pinned to a tree,
Is a set of by-laws, one of which
Prohibits the landing of aircraft
In the village, another the climbing of trees.

Then, in a space defined by an absence
Of sheep, where flocks are gathered
In August, a man comes running at me,
In wellingtons, his flies undone,

A mobile in his succinct fist,
And asks me if I've seen the helicopter,
Which I have. It landed outside
The village, behind some Christmas trees,

I can still hear its knife-and-fork din,
And he runs gratefully towards it
Without telling us who is suffering;
Later we heard the rotor ascending.

Porch Swallows

In a nest no bigger than the breast pocket
Of your old art teacher's tweed jacket
They are raising a family, biro-black and bubble-eyed,
Blind when we came here.

She climbs a coiled path of air
And picks berries of blood from it,
Chucks herself back and banks on a pinhead,
Whiplashes in at the porch, up to its nook,

Then sticks heartwrung mites into a set
Of mouths agape as bells.
And we are in muscle-agony on a col,
Toiling up a one-in-three.

By nighttime she sits on her lot
Like the lid of a brown betty,
Settles herself on a cache of knife-edge wings,
Doesn't flinch in the dazzling wink

Of my late night torch. All I see
Is a kind of shadow play, a tiny head
Made huge on a riddled eave,
While directly below on the flag

A berg of droppings grows like pottery,
A stalagmite still warm, like the bottle
We try not to kick on our way out,
And which is full every morning.

Air

I woke up in a chilled bed
Convinced, beyond all reason,
That the coolant in the air-con system
Was water that had been used
To wash the bodies of the victims,
Those poor things we'd cried about
When we saw them on the local news,
Laid out in rows on the lacquered floor
Of the gymnasium, whose expressions
Of bloody peacefulness the camera,
Even here, shied away from.

On a Photograph of My Mother Expecting Me

An afternoon of Coca-Cola and birdsong,
Beneath the poplar that would fall
And fall and fall again.

I'm surprised I'm not American
With that classic bottle in your hand
And all that sugar in our blood,

To be nurtured on such a kick
Of sugar and sugar and sugar again
Must leave its mark.

The whole thing fell but just missed me,
Like the house in that Buster Keaton
Flick, when he survives the crashing wall

By standing still, exactly where
The little window touches ground.
At least he knew what was coming,

And in all those walls that fell,
We were saved by windows as well,
Though they were shut, and we had to breach

Their frosted panes, like candy glass
Cracked over our crowns, the bottles
That broke and broke and broke again.

A Poodle Symposium

First proof – that they snap, and can draw blood.
No hypothetical dog can do this.
That they look like ghosts is no evidence that they are.
There are many of them, too many, but that each
Is owned and accounted for by a distinct individual.
They are dogs of flesh and blood and wool.
They appear to be able to leap out of their own bodies.
They are sculpted like privet or yew.

Second proof. They were here before us.
They have their own will, and won't perform feats
Simply as a result of your willing them to do so.
They look like thoughts.
They can dance.
They look like clouds, and can rain.
They can turn on a sixpence.
They look like noughts.
A litter of clouds can look like a fleet of poodles.

Third proof. We've forgotten what we're trying to prove.
They look like Marie Antoinette.
Their tails are triple-topiaried, with extra pom-poms
And pompadours.

Fourth proof. If they didn't exist, then the Poodle Parlour
On the Parade would pass out of existence also,
And my mother works in there.

Fifth proof. Our husbands are becoming more fastidious.
They park symmetrically;
Their parking is a ballet of automobiles,
They have taken to taming the hedges, the privet,
It no longer blooms, they are seeing themselves
In poodle-light, they even begin to walk as lightly,
On the front of the foot, I've seen it. Nothing
Immaterial could cause this

Sixth proof. The owner of the Poodle Parlour
(Which exists) is called Pierre, a retired acrobat.
We've seen poodles come all flowing-
Shanked and flossy-muzzled from there. He is a man
Of stout morals, clipper-sure, a good scissorboy.
You'd trust him with your most precious beard.

Seventh proof. A proof by elimination.
Because Mrs Spoke claimed hers had the gift
Of languages, and could turn invisible at will,
That it was an indestructible lap dog . . .

Eighth proof. That they fight, and in fighting
Inadvertently perform the death scene from
Swan Lake. And that I've seen them
Doubled in puddles, trembling in Manchester breezes,
(To tremble is a sure proof of existence).
Poodles tip-toeing over zebra crossings (implicit, explicit),
They are dogs on sticks, candy floss,
Earthbound clouds, Galateas
Of the balloon magician.
What – you don't believe us?
I know. Just when they seemed so real
Just when they promised to be with us
You touch them, like hoar frost
They're gone.

Poodles *a priori*. Elemental poodles. Empirical poodles

Ninth proof   Prof

                             poodle

    Poof

                    Pop

On Certain Problems with the New Body-Suits

It was that time of year when the bears were held to account.
The costumes now were so good you couldn't tell
Just by looking deep in the spinal fur for a zip, nor by smelling
For the meaty breath, nor by looking into the brownsome eyes
To see if anything of intelligence lived within the glass
Then wrestle with an inner demon who cries "Get off, you cunt!"

Then does a hatchet job with a pad of fives – so splayed
And to the point you carry a tic tac toe of blood on your cheek
That'll have your missus begging you to take a week off work,
As if you could afford to go on the sick with the rates what
    they are,
You'll take anything that's given. You'll tell her it's like a holy war
In which neither side has any religion – but you both get paid.

It was like we had to separate the bear-sheep from the bear-goats
When they raided the supermarkets for copies of *Take a Break*
And *WordSearch Weekly*, the Sudoku games in *TV Quick*.
You might have thought the bear impersonators were at the till
And that the checkout girls were safe, you might have thought
    that until
The very moment when the grizzlies swiped their cards across
    their throats.

It's no longer possible to tell, now they've developed an interest in
     puzzles,
Gained the powers of eloquence that has them reeling off jokes
In the queues for the loos; we used to think that that's what makes
Us human, reading the funnies, but now the only sure way
Is a flashlight down the throat, or an analysis of their wee,
A swab of their rectal opening, a cotton bud probe of their
     muzzles,

Or a scan with the infra-red, which could separate the imposter
From his costume, the ghost from the machine, though even that
Was old hat these days, giving only one burning silhouette.
I thought I should give it up, after I'd nearly lost a finger
To a certain sow I was sure contained my ex, she was a ringer
And I made my final deposition with all the energy I could muster

To Soothe the Last Moments of a Dying Man

From the Assyrian

We steeped several handkerchiefs in important perfumes,
Tied each with seven knots, and bound them
Round his head, and round his wrists and ankles,
Like soft manacles or fetters. We sprinkled his body
With bright wine, and sang quiet songs.
Later we described the house he would live in
When all this was over.

Hanging

i.m. Michael Donaghy

What a fucking liberty
To stake my claim and use you
As a way of remembering myself.
Well, it's all about taking liberties
Isn't it, this business? We can't
Have met more than a dozen times.

One of them being in the week
Michael Hutchence died, found hanging
From a wardrobe door, like a tie. Not a very
Rock and Roll death, we thought,
Not like choking on your own vomit
While going down in a plane

That crashes into a swimming pool.
I can number them – (1) the evening spent
At your downstairs flat in the road
That was on the edge of my own
Old manor, named for a forgotten field marshal.
You put all our names through

The spellcheck on your Amstrad
So that I was reborn as Geared Woodland,
(A shady character), and the last time (12)
Must have been that Arts Council hand-out night
When we were both in luck,
With friends on the panel.

You greeted me with your conjuror's handshake
And told a long, complicated, unfunny
But brilliant joke which, like the handshake,
Was a way of drawing the unravelled string
Of our tension into a ball that would fit
Easily into your pocket.

We both went home richer
That night, and should have celebrated,
Though you probably did, hard
And for too long. I left you strap-hanging
On the northbound tube, smiling abstractedly
And bound for my own old manor.

Taking the Measure

(an inappropriation, written on the occasion of the retirement of
Professor Richard Francis)

'Sewall enjoyed measuring public buildings with his joint rule'
– Richard Francis, *Judge Sewall's Apology*

Pioneering tourism in the Newton Park Estate, where his father
Had once thought about being the parson, before
Thinking better of it, Samuel Sewall indulged his great passion
For measurement, unfolding the knuckles of his rule
With an efficient clickety-clack, and exclaiming with joy
A few busy minutes later; that the church of the Holy Trinity
Was exactly fifty yards in length and thirty wide by its
Transepts, that the schoolhouse had a width of fifteen yards
And seven inches, that the bakery was five yards wide
And seven yards long and that the blacksmith's was exactly
Twenty feet from end to end. "O the wonder of establishing
The dimensions of a thing, the joy of it. To know how something
Measures up is to possess it, in a way." The blacksmith
Remarked that this was a very pertinent point indeed,
And so did the blacksmith's wife. "He gaineth three inches
Every morn," she remarked, "which is quite gone by
Breakfast time. I cannot fathom his perpetual lengthening
And shortening, perhaps you could help?" "Are we talking
Appurtenances of the masculine gender?" Samuel enquired.
"I have no idea," replied the blacksmith's wife, "though
If you wouldn't mind witnessing the moment, you could

At least confirm the phenomenon for me." So Samuel Sewall
Found himself spending an unusual night between the blacksmith
And his wife, in the scrolled iron bed that the man himself
Had wrought, Samuel's joint rule folded chastely and held like
A crucifix to his breast, while the burning breath of the blacksmith
Swept over him in molten waves. As the cock crew, and the sun
Sewed its dazzling embroidery, Sewall began unfolding
His joint rule, just as the blacksmith began unfolding himself
And, measure for measure, he found the blacksmith
Was extended a full nine inches from root to crown,
That made the visitor cry out in astonishment, which begat
A rather unfortunate sequence of events. The blacksmith
With dreamy arousal and eyes still closed, went down
To take hold of himself – instead he grasped the visitor's
Measure, rolled onto his side and with quiet murmurs
Of delight, buggered poor Samuel to a depth of ten inches.

Jackdaws

They have a journalist's interest
In things thrown away.
They have an inner eyelid
But no inner eye.

They gut our rubbish,
Strew it across the yard.
They edit out what is edible,
Leave the letters from the credit card

People, the blister packs, the Lil-lets;
Our story, but then they take
These too. It's spring. Nests
Have to be built, the muckrake

Stowed for another season.
I can hear them gossiping in the poplar,
They've woven my wife's
Blood into their wallpaper,

They've used dosage charts
To line their cots –
What input for their children.
What else do they know about us? Hacks!

Regiment des Dromadaires

'Neither meals nor lovemaking should last
More than a quarter of an hour'
– Napoleon

We were not wanted but we came anyway
Arriving on novel forms of transport.
Our legs had no more strength
Than ribbons of knotted silk.

We carried the desert on our tongues,
Upended our moaning beasts in the main square,
Filled ourselves at the fountain
Until someone cried out that it tasted of blood.
And true, the cistern, we later found,
Was filled to its lip with the heads
Of nearly a hundred unidentified females.

The general shook out a tablecloth.
The trees shook out their orioles.
Later, he asked my opinion of his new attire.
For a small man he carried himself well, though I strained to
    hold my laughter.

The lecture on fish didn't go down well.
"It is known that God created precisely thirty thousand types
    of animal,"
A man from the audience interrupted, "Ten thousand on land,
Twenty thousand in the water.
There is nothing more to be said."

Two or three puppeteers
And some iron foundrymen
Were playing *vingt et un* outside an undertaker's.

It was left to the aeronaut Conte
To turn things around.
He proposed an ascent in a paper balloon.

In an opal twilight his craft carried
Over the roof of the Institute, and sailed
Towards the Barkiya Hills.
Then, it seemed, a new star had appeared in the east.
His ash took a week to reach us.

Reflux

At night the anglers pass
Beneath my window,
Taking the quickest way

To the reservoir
Where they'll not sleep
But sit on folding nylon chairs

In the gaze of a small Gaz
Lantern, catching twenty-five pounds
Of moonlight on their lines,

And waiting for the bite
Of the fish that have climbed
The famous ladder of drinking water.

At dawn, if I'm still here,
They'll pass again, more slowly,
More laden. They'll feel it

By then, the sleeplessness,
Just as I'll feel the acid
Tipping into my throat.

An Insult

(after Patrick Kavanagh)

I came to a great house at the edge of a park,
Unsure if this was where I was meant to be.
I could hear the sneezing of the swans
On the folded-up lake, it was like the whole
World was stretched out and drunk on a lawn.
The lawn on which, now, a man was giving his all
To the task of preserving a shark.
Out on the lawn, beneath the portioned glaze
Of thirteen good windows, he was doing this thing
Of preserving a shark, a great white, in a tank
Of formaldehyde. He had a crane, as tall
And as tapered as a redwood, (though with a dangerous
Lean), mounted on the back of a lorry
From *Thunderbirds*, with four twenty-foot stabilizers
Planted square on the ground (half on the grass, half
On the drive), and from this the shark hung –
Above the shrubberies, above the sundials,
Above the topiary chess pieces, above
The stacked stripes of the near-perfect
Viridian lawn, revolving solemnly in its sling
On the light torque of a steel cable, its mouth slightly open
And full of that surprising, frightening and yet-
What-else-were-you-expecting thing – teeth.

There was a crowd to one side of the lawn,
An audience of sorts, though not of fans. In fact
They were protesters against cruelty to animals.
The shark, they said, had been shot for no other purpose
Than to furnish this tank. An insult. They were behind ropes,
Kettled between the house and the orangery
By a picket of riot police, for their own safety,
They said. The whole lot could come down
At any moment – the crane tip, the shark swing
Like a wrecking ball swallowing everything in its path.
No one was buying it, and then one of them got through,
A kid in a mohawk and shredded jeans, unnoticed
Until she was up to the glass of the tank when,
As if by some conjuring trick, she produced
An improbably long and heavy sledgehammer
And, taking a well-judged swing at the vat
Smashed through three inches of glass and let gush
(At such pressure it swept herself, the artist,
The crane operator, two peacocks and a photographer
Away across the lawn in several directions),
Four hundred and forty-seven gallons of formaldehyde.

That wasn't the end of it, though by now
I had passed beyond the house and the lawn. I wondered
What formaldehyde did to grass – kill it, or
Preserve it for ever? And the shark, how long
Could it hang there in the dirty summer air?
In the end I wasn't sure there was an answer,
All I could do was hope for guidance through the park,
And to be silent until I was out of it.

Launch

i.m. Mick Imlah

It was one of your standard jokes
When at a launch or something similar,
To ask the poet if you could look
At their newly minted book,
Then, after a moment's thoughtful reading,
Make as if to hurl it out of the deep
Into a distant wicket keeper's exaggerated hands.

A clumsy way of bringing poetry and sport
Together, but not as bad as that other trick of yours
When handed a precious volume
To suddenly run with it as though
You'd taken a blinding pass
With a man over and forty yards to the line,
Challenging the poet to a pursuit if he dared,

A tackle, even. You tried it once with me on the Strand,
Ran so far you actually went out of sight.
You were a little disappointed, I know,
When I declined the chase and followed
At a walking amble to find you loitering,
Smiling, puzzled beneath St Clement Danes,
The book you'd edited now limp in your hands.

But I could never have caught you up.
In truth I was shocked by this sudden burst
Of horseplay from one so mild, so quiet.
It was one of your many surprising sides, like that one
I saw pasted on the starboard of a London bus,
Near Charing Cross, en route to our first proper meeting,
An ad for GAP, that nearly knocked me down,

I didn't know you'd reached those heights – model, moodily lit,
Well-togged. You got paid in clothes
For that stand-in job. How easily you fell
Into that role, (but then – you were beautiful).
And yet how ill at ease you could seem
In the canaped world of a book launch.
The grimace you gave when informed

By the hosts that you were expected
To do the intros. *Can't we just toast*
The poets and give them three cheers
And have done with the rest, I imagined
You thinking. Well. Here is my book.
I'd like you to put it on a spot of turf
In line with an almighty H, and launch it.

Crimes Against the Ox

(from the laws drawn up by King Hammurabi of Babylon in 1750 BC)

248

If anyone hire an ox and break off a horn, or cut off its tail or hurt its muzzle, he shall pay one fourth of its value in money to the owner.

249

No man should kill an ox before the end of its working life. If he do, he will be yoked, and will draw a plough, a day for every year of the ox.

250

No man should attempt to seduce a woman by means of feeding he warm tripe, if this is the sole reason for the killing of an ox.

251

Any game of football will be declared void and the teams suspended if it is discovered that the ball is the bladder of an ox.

252

If an ox be a goring ox, and it shown that he is a gorer, and he do not bind his horns, or fasten the ox up, and the ox gore a free-born man and kill him, the owner shall pay a one-half mina in money.

253

It is forbidden to set alight the tail of an ox.

254

It is forbidden to wrestle within view of an ox.

255

It is forbidden to dress an ox in any form of apparel.

256

A menstruating woman should not be placed upwind of an untethered ox.

257

It is forbidden to give lectures, if such lectures entail the chalking of words or mathematical symbols on the side of an ox.

258

It is forbidden to serve a Sunday dinner with an ox in lieu of a table.

259

It is forbidden to make a large number of people laugh out loud by means of ridiculing an ox.

260

It is forbidden to swing from the horns of an ox, or to conspire to cause others to so swing, or to make plans (diagrams, drawings, models etc) to this end, or to think about making such plans.

261

No man should bring mirrors to bear upon an ox, if the intention is to confuse, belittle or embarrass the ox.

262

Law number 260 also applies to the tail.

263

It is forbidden to conduct loud conversation within earshot of an ox, unless the ox be acknowledged.

264

An ox should not be given use of a telescope.

265

Law number 260 also applies to the organs of generation.

266

It is forbidden knowingly to bring an ox into a state of disappointment.

My Lemon and Ginger Infusion

I know I've always feared the worst,
Losing my life, losing my mind,
My lemon and ginger infusion has burst.

You could say that my breakfast was cursed,
That my eggs were doomed, by bacon ruined,
I know I've always feared the worst.

It just seems such a terrible waste,
Those roots and seeds floating around,
My lemon and ginger infusion has burst.

You tell me it's all like grist
To my mill, but I'm a ship that's run aground.
I know I've always feared the worst.

And I had such a godawful thirst,
So I drink your tea (you don't mind),
My lemon and ginger infusion has burst.

It's all a matter of trust.
Now it's broken I feel I've drowned.
I know I've always feared the worst,
My lemon and ginger infusion has burst.

The Longjumellois

In Lauderdale, Minnesota
I dreamt that I had passed away
And was taking dinner with the dead.

They said they came from Lonjumeau
And we drank to the health of the Longjumellois

"Leave electricity to the electricians . . ."

An orchid springs back
Like a snapped rubber band.

Here you can breathe
Ten different kinds of air,
More than can be sipped
On all the quays of Connecticut

Matteo Liviero

An extra-solar planet
Orbiting a numbered star
In the constellation of the Sextant

Moves at such a lick
It is like watching the midfielder
Matteo Liviero of Juventus kick

An Earth-defying, sweet, curving
Ball that cuts a defence
In two. It's that same swing

That, in Corinth, brought the hollow
Cry from those surviving —
Fall, I will follow.

Brambles

i.m. Peter Redgrove.

Mid-June on a disused railway, now a cycle-path,
During a difficult few days of hot weather,
And a long agonizing walk through South Manchester,
In a cutting I came across a crowd of brambles
Filling its south-facing slope, so that my view
Was upwards across petal-heads towards blue sky.
They were taking the full weight of the sun,
The flowers candy-pink, bright as coins,
With here and there the green gesture
Of a stalk reaching beyond, and everywhere bees
Nuzzling down, bending then straightening their aching backs
Like old geezers on their allotments.
Inching closer, treading with the caution of a late arrival
In a theatre, I could see in each flower, behind
A kind of false moustache, the fruit-to-be,
Still sap-tight, scrunched up discretely
Like a boy's scrotum. They were inviting, like the sea.
Something to wade into, or a pink fluffy carpet
On which to pad barefoot to heaven.
Though I soon sensed how I was being seen through.
It was the sun they were interested in, an attentive audience
To its solar acrobatics, its slow, graceful leap
Through a hoop of its own flame, I was suspended
In their silent applause, the cheering beyond hearing
And understood how a walk on that succulent pile

Would be to sink hip-deep in teeth, to be eaten
Like children are in their dreams by greenish dragons.
They would savage me for the protection of their
Pollinated broods, and before I'd got to the top my flesh
Would have been picked out, scooped up, hung on a thousand
Dainty hooks, they might strip me down to a drifting core
Of spirit, wardrobe my flesh in leafy wardrobes,
And have the wasps and flesh-flies paddle in my blood on its
        platters,
Then those Salomes to come in the heel of summer
When they take the heads of the fruit in which I'm implicated,
To fill their Kwik Save carrier bags with gore, and then an
        autumn
Spent in slow boiling against my own weight in sugar,
And the promise of my bleeding again in afternoons to come,
Lying painlessly wounded on the back of a child's finger,
Mistaken for blood and kissed away.

Life In the House to be Demolished

She said "You are like a cow that has strayed
Through a gap in the fence and can't find a way back in,
But instead of revelling in your newfound freedom

You sulk in a space you cannot comprehend."
She had a point. For a long time I'd wondered
How the cows managed without any form of shelter

Other than a half shattered and scatter-leafed oak,
With nothing for them to go inside, nor anything
From which they can emerge, and I thought

That I might end up in similar straits
When the house in which I lived was finally
Demolished. Cows have no desire for escape

Because they don't understand that they are confined;
You don't see them gathered at a field gate trying
To puzzle out the latch, or work their tongue

On a sprung handle, though those organs can seem
As prehensile as hands. Their lives are conducted
Through a system of doors, opening and closing,

For no purpose that they can discern.
She mentioned this aspect, and suggested I consider
My life in the house to be demolished part of a similar

Masterplan of which I could have no understanding.
Think of those walls coming down simply as vast doors
(Doors as big as walls), opening.

I thought of telling her about the walk I took
Along the lane above the fields from which I could
Look down and saw, to my surprise, that the cows

Had arranged themselves in the field in such a way
That they formed the numeral 2, which for two mad minutes
I believed represented the time left till doomsday,

(And what should I do when that hour comes,
Carve the word *adieu* into every corner of my trembling house,
Strip it bare and run naked from the open door as the
     wrecking ball

Makes its final approach – jump and cling to it like a baby
     chimpanzee?)
Thinking of my house in cow terms, she said, has become
One of my most disagreeable habits; she meant the theory I had

That one's life, at any given moment, is a miraculous
Jig saw that just happened to fall into its own solution,
In the way that cows will come together to pass through a gate,

Or flow down a lane, like a barge passing through a lock,
But a barge that can dissolve into fragments at any moment.
The house is like that, a collection of small things

That have fallen into place, but only for the micro-moment
Of my residence. So life in the house to be demolished
Has become a sort of prayer of thanks

To the gods of tessellation, who gaze upon us
With their Rubik's cube faces. And the upshot
Of this was that I invited the cows in.

They are such near neighbours
That stepping over the threshold didn't seem
Such a big deal, their voices were already in the house.

They traipsed in through the patio doors,
Like hoodies in a church, bashful and uncomprehending,
Sweeping ornaments from the mantelpiece with a casual turn of
    the head

Letting form instantly small circular rugs of themselves
On the carpet, then trailing their glossy spittle,
Lacing my hardware with it, suddenly bolting

Into the false dawn of a mirror, and breaking it.
And so an uneasy menage was formed,
The cows stayed downstairs, I lived upstairs,

And we shared the kitchen,
(Though the cows preferred the garden during the day).
Do I ever need to worry about milk again?

(No – I didn't worry about it in the first place).
We spent our evenings breaking things.
But it wasn't long before they were complaining,

Producing long, foggy moans whenever the television
Lurched into a commercial break, and they threw back at me
Whatever tray of goodies I brought, said they couldn't sleep

On my lumpy bed. They have eaten my alarm clock.
Such attitudes. Such tedious stories. The aurochs –
Who cares? The last survivors were hunted into a ditch,

They tell me. A little herd lived on into the seventeenth century
On a chilly estate in Poland. Perhaps they'll dig one up
And take a pinch of DNA from its marrow, I suggested.

This caused a teacup to burst into stars above my head.
We have upholstered the thrones of kings
Since the time of Tiglath-Pileser I, they informed me, who hunted

The aurochs for kudos, and for something to go
On his mantelpiece. O the bother of endowing cows
With a sense of history. They had the whole domestication thing

Down pat – how it was engineered by the continual separation
Of herds, until the will of Taurus had been unspliced
From his body, to leave these, a race of mothers who lived

In fear and trembling, protein-reservoirs, wet-nurses,
Who act out the sadness of Niobe in their barbed-wire palaces,
Whose true gift to the human race is tuberculosis . . .

I told them they were making my life intolerable,
And stamped across the lane and into their vacated field.
I stood it for an hour in sheeting rain,

It was like walking on a giant solitaire board,
Up to my ankles in their hoofsteps. In the great
Quadrilateral I felt like crying to the heavens

For something more enclosing, and conceded
I had learnt something about the life of cows,
How they can stand out there even while the frost

Is doing its applique, how every night for them
Is a version of Lear's elemental madness,
How they are lit up by lightning glaring through

The fork of an oak, have jackdaws walking
The notched tightropes of their spines every morning,
And live on a carpet of their entire cuisine.

I gave up and plodded back but, you've guessed it,
The walls had come down about the twitching ears
Of my cow tenants, they'd wrecked it themselves,

No need for crews in hard hats. They stood as solid
And as squarely upright as tables amid the crumbs of my house,
I tried a tit-for-tat, but all I could do

Was swipe at the air. I'm sorry,
I was too overcome to even think
About what I was seeing. You've watched this sort of thing

On the news, haven't you? You've seen the cows
Wrecking other lives, and you think it will
Never happen to you. But it will. I must go now.

ACKNOWLEDGEMENTS

Some of these poems first appeared in *New Welsh Review*.
'Taking the Measure' first appeared in *Heavy Dancing, Writing for
Richard Francis*. An earlier version of 'A Poodle Symposium' appeared
in *Boomerang*. The author would like to thank Bath Spa University
for their sabbatical, and Columbia College Chicago for their writer in
residency, during which this collection was finished. Many thanks to
friends, colleagues and students at both institutions, and especially
to Tim Liardet.